W9-BCR-469

Published by
Princeton Architectural Press
A McEvoy Group company
202 Warren Street, Hudson, NY 12534
Visit our website at www.papress.com

© 2018 Brad Holdgrafer and Jay Cover
All rights reserved
Printed in China by C&C Offset Printing Co., Ltd.
21 20 19 18 4 3 2 1 First edition

Princeton Architectural Press is a leading publisher in architecture, design,
photography, landscape, and visual culture. We create fine books and stationery
of unsurpassed quality and production values. With more than one thousand titles
published, we find design everywhere and in the most unlikely places.

No part of this book may be used or reproduced in any manner without written
permission from the publisher, except in the context of reviews.

Every reasonable attempt has been made to identify owners of copyright.
Errors or omissions will be corrected in subsequent editions.

The book was illustrated using graphite, Letraset, and digital color.

Editor: Nina Pick
Typesetting: Paul Wagner

Special thanks to: Ryan Alcazar, Paula Baver, Janet Behning, Abby Bussel,
Benjamin English, Jan Cigliano Hartman, Susan Hershberg, Kristen Hewitt,
Lia Hunt, Valerie Kamen, Simone Kaplan-Senchak, Jennifer Lippert, Sara McKay,
Eliana Miller, Nina Pick, Wes Seeley, Rob Shaeffer, Sara Stemen, Marisa Tesoro,
and Joseph Weston of Princeton Architectural Press
—Kevin C. Lippert, publisher

Library of Congress Cataloging-in-Publication Data
Names: Holdgrafer, Brad, author. | Cover, Jay, illustrator.
Title: Walls / Brad Holdgrafer and Jay Cover.
Description: First edition. | Hudson, NY : Princeton Architectural Press,
  a McEvoy Group company, [2018]
Identifiers: LCCN 2017055180 | ISBN 9781616897093
Subjects: LCSH: Interpersonal relations—Juvenile literature. | Social
  integration—Juvenile literature. | Social conflict—Juvenile literature.
  | Walls—Juvenile literature.
Classification: LCC HM1106 .H636 2018 | DDC 302—dc23
LC record available at https://lccn.loc.gov/2017055180

WALLS

Written by **Brad Holdgrafer**   Illustrated by **Jay Cover**

PRINCETON ARCHITECTURAL PRESS · NEW YORK

Some walls are made
for animal farms,
to keep the farm animals
from animal harm.

For the cows and the pigs
and the veggies too,
these walls at the farm
are no cause for alarm.

Some walls are
made for sports,
to keep bouncing balls
inside the court.

To the players, the coaches,
their fans, and their friends,
these walls are
a court's support of sorts.

9

Some blank walls
are made for art.
Finished art or art
you still mean to start.

With pencils or brushes
or even a lemon tart!
It doesn't matter what art
if it comes from the heart.

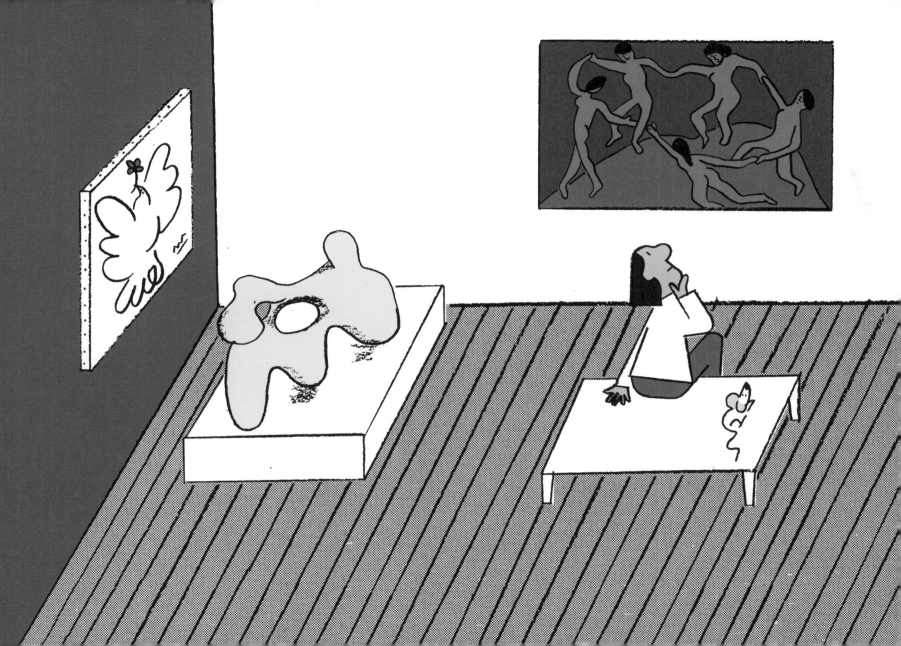

Some four walls
are made for houses.
Not four houses but
FOR HOUSES!

Like yours, your friends',
and your neighbors' too.
Even a mouse needs walls
in his house.

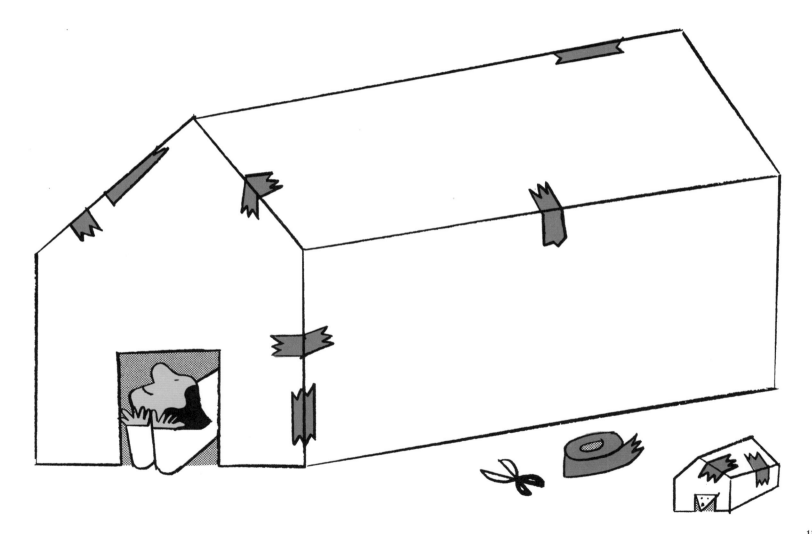

13

But then there are walls
that cast shadows over all.
You know the kind,
big as waterfalls.

Walls so tall you can't
hear a friend call.
These tall walls we like
least of all.

They keep out the people
we'd like to meet,
or who'd like to meet us,
if it weren't for concrete!

These walls are unfriendly,
and perhaps even rude.
They block new adventures
with their bad attitude.

We just don't like
these kinds of walls.
We just don't like
these walls at all.

So, even if your hands
are small, go stand
on the tallest of walls
and call!

THESE

ARE THE WALL^S
WE LIKE LEAST OF ALL!
THESE are the WALLS
WE LIKE LEAST OF ALL!

THESE ARE THE WALLS WE LIKE
LEAST OF ALL!

And if we all yell at once,
then our voices get loud.

See!
One, two, and three.
Now, that's a real crowd!

And those big, boring walls,
they'll soon tumble down,
so exciting new friends can start
to come 'round.

Different kinds of people,
all working together.

Now, that's the sort of thinking that makes the world better.

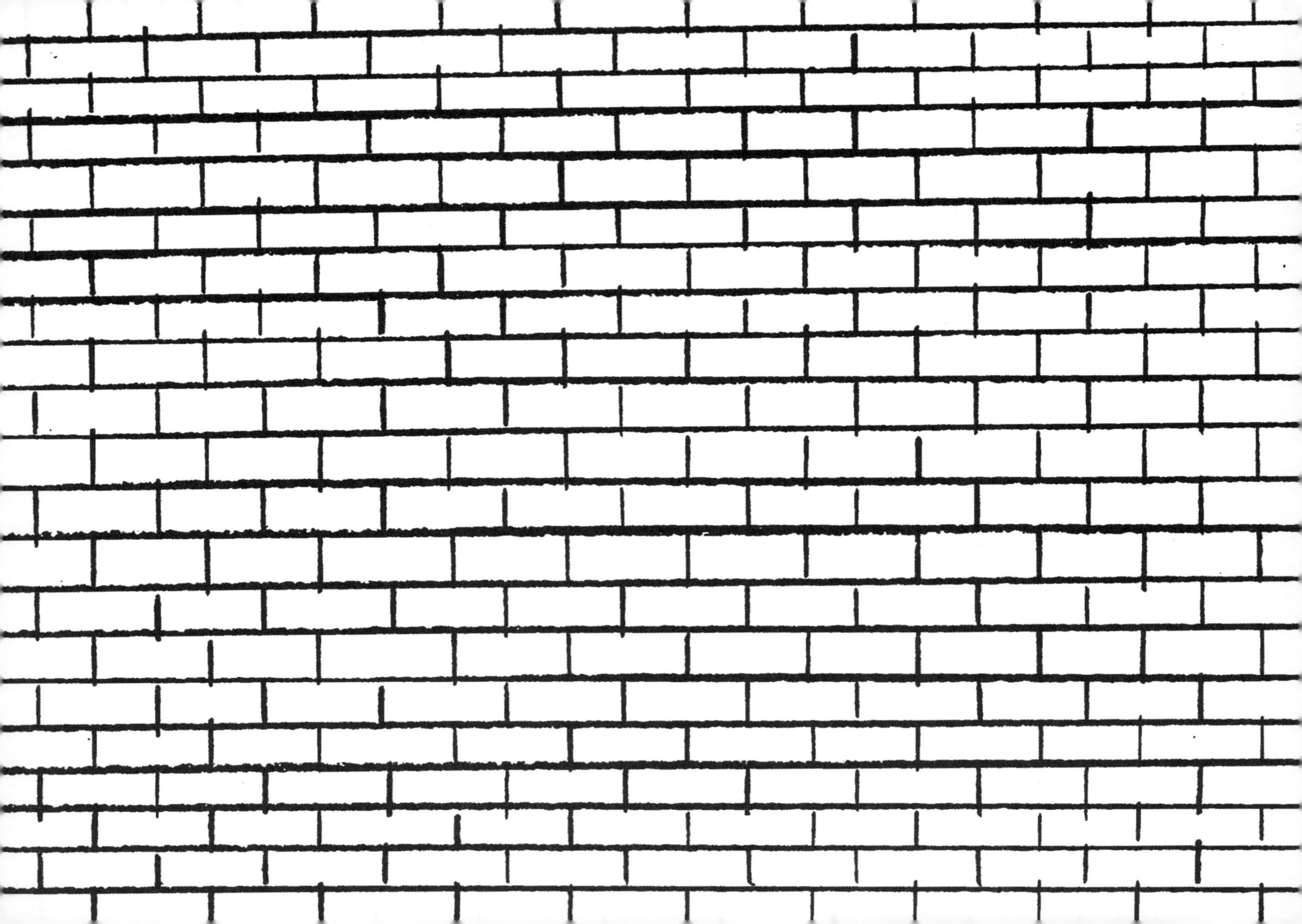